Enabled

Ruth Merry
Steve Emecz

From Ruth to;

Mum, Dad, Sarah, Linda, Cheryl, Kris, Auntie Rosalie, Pam, Janye, the Paone family, David, and all my friends and family... also to Andy, Steve and Onno who wanted to be as crazy as me.

This book tells the true story of how one disabled lady's dream to defy her disability and tackle something most people would think impossible. It's told from two perspectives – her own, and that of her 'able-bodied' friend who made the rollercoaster journey with her. Let's meet the two of them and the two lads that came along for the ride.

Ruth (aka Ruthie/Rufus/Speedy/Binky)

Despite having to deal with Arthrogryposis (which affects her joints, muscles and nerve endings) Ruth has always lived her life large and she doesn't like to feel anything has beaten her. With the support of her family and friends she competed for many years in her favourite sports of swimming, skiing, athletics and horse riding. Although she retired from competitive sport several years ago, in between working full time she describes herself as always looking for a new and exciting adventure.

Steve (aka The Puppy)

As a gym teacher's son, and with two brothers, Steve had no option but to be active. Whatever sport with bat or ball Steve grew up running, hitting competing and enjoying sport. By the time he met Ruth through work Steve had reached the dreaded thirty years old and left it behind with a defining moment that would give them a common bond – the New York Marathon in 2001. Steve ran the marathon for a mobility disability charity called Leonard Cheshire and ended up sharing a room with one of the charity's centre manager's – something that would change Steve's views on disability dramatically. From that moment on Steve pledged to do something for the charity every year. In 2002 the London Triathlon, in 2003 the European Lake race and in 2005 the Triathlon and the Nottingham Marathon. Our story starts a couple of months before the London Triathlon in 2005.

Onno (aka The Flying Dutchman)

Works with Ruth and Steve. Lives in Holland and is the team's resident extreme sports nut, from high speed snowboarding to kite surfing. Onno also keeps fit by teaching 'spinning'. He travels to the UK every week to spend time with the team, and the rest of the time jets around Europe helping put the 'e' in e-commerce.

Andy H (aka Stretch)

Steve's 6'5" best friend and always up to join in on any adventure going. Andy works for a large airline, lives in London and supplements his daily use of public transport with throwing a TVR [Brit Supercar] around the countryside at the weekends. Ideal qualifications to be involved in an escapade that involves speed and travel.

[Brit Supercar] TVRs are hand made British supercars that have 400 horsepower yet weigh less than the average contestant on Celebrity Fit Club. 0-60pmh in 4 seconds. Quick.

Chapter 1 – Impossible Challenge

June 2005 – Monday

Steve

It's another Monday and I'm already tired – stuck in a traffic jam on the way to work. Yesterday's run with Andy was as competitive as ever and the nine miles really took it out of me. I know it's good for my training to be doing it with my best friend but I didn't realise we would push each other so much. At least it should have a positive effect on my Triathlon time. I hate running mainly because I'm not good at it. Being quite thick set, due to being a swimmer when I was a child, I seem to bulk up when I train and I can't seem to increase my running speed higher than a gentle plod. How well I'll get on in the marathon with Andy in Nottingham in September is a concern. Looks like there's a small accident on the A414 and its going to take me another half an hour extra to get into work today, which I can really do without as there's a new project going live this week. I guess it will be a takeaway tonight if Sharon's working late as well.

Ruth

Woke up after a broken night of sleep. My body is on strike again and not wanting to work. It's going to take a while to get going this morning. Stuff the damp, cold, British weather. The sooner I get back to California, the happier I'll be – the drier climate suits me better. I start rocking from side to side to start the process of getting out of bed. I laugh at myself as I remember what Linda said to me about the way I have to get out of bed. "Ruthie, you have a strange way of praying" the laughing and memory takes my mind off the fact that my right hip has cracked and is hurting. I eventually make it to the bathroom and end up doing my impression of Torvill and Dean and Peggy Flemming across the floor while transferring from my wheelchair to the loo. I give myself a six for artistic impression.

Steve
Into the office in Hemel Hempstead and the morning ritual of getting in the coffee. The first into the office is normally Malcolm – you can tell if he's around as there is a fresh pot. No Malcolm then. Dave and Sandra will have tea, and I'd probably do the same but Ruth likes her filter coffee so I'd better put one on.

Ruth
I'm going to have to phone Dave to come and open the doors again. The outer door is stuck and isn't opening up with the pass. Wait a minute, a bit of luck someone's coming. It's one of the young lads from the call centre and he pulls open the doors and lets me in. That's lucky – I know he doesn't mind but I feel bad disturbing Dave every time this happens. Dave sees me in the corridor and gives me a push up the slope into the office. I wheel round the corner and as usual Steve's desk is the first one I pass on my way through to the desk I have by the window. I always like to say hello to Steve on the way in. He's my boss's boss by the way, but I've known him for quite a few years since he worked in the UK supplies section.

"You look tired Steve, heavy one on the booze eh?"

"Oh yeah, eight pints just before my training run on Sunday – should have thought of that". Steve always jokes about his training. He's not a natural athlete bless him but he tries hard. I decide to wind him up on the fundraising.

"You can borrow my spare chair if you like, if you promise not to race it. That's the problem with you though Steve, you're always very selfish with your fundraising"

"OK. I guess you're going to explain just how that is?"

"Every year it's the same, you pick something that only you can do – deliberately discriminating against me so I can't take part. You know I can't do marathons and Triathlons. See, selfish". I can't help laughing as I try to give Steve an evil stare.

"Well ok. How about this then. You can choose whatever you like for next year and we'll do it together."

"Anything?" I grin as I lift myself up in my chair to see Steve's face over the partition.

"Yep. Anything you like" Steve smiles.

"OK". I think for a moment. "Let's do a Bobsleigh".

Steve hesitates. "A Bobsleigh. As in run alongside and jump in Bobsleigh?". His face is a picture.

"You did say anything". I'm insistent and stubborn. I used to ski a lot when I was younger and the one thing I always dreamed of was the Bobsleigh. It was one of the events that the disabled athletes didn't take part in. I'd seen many tracks around the world when I was competing and there was something about the speed that was very exciting.

"Well, I'll see what I can do" Steve says. It's a good joke and I'm sure he takes it the way it's meant. I think we will end up doing a sponsored swim together this year. I was pretty fast in my day and even held a world record at one point. Bit slower these days but I'm probably still faster than Steve.

Steve
Bobsleigh. Good one. Ruth always makes me smile. I plough into the stack of emails that have come in during the evening from the US on the programs I'm working on and rapidly the Europeans add to the pile. The Fins are two hours ahead of us and ironically for a small country they have ended up with some big contracts so although I'm in from 7am most days that's 9am for them so they are well into the swing by the time I have got half way through my first cup of coffee.

'Lunchtime' arrives – an interesting concept which basically means a wolfed sandwich at my desk and a few minutes looking at a couple of things for the upcoming Triathlon. The charity loves it when we can squeeze some press coverage by doing something silly. This year we have set up a website called 'Fat Boy Slims' and are having a competition between me and Andy on who loses the most weight. We're pretty level at the moment with a couple of stone each. Ruth's Bobsleigh idea is niggling at my brain so I do a quick Google search and find that there are about 20 tracks around the world and it doesn't take 15 minutes to email them all asking on the off chance did they have a program to let the public try the Bob out and in particular was there accommodation for disabled people. At least I'll be able to say I gave it a go.

By mid afternoon several of the tracks have responded. Not surprisingly they are pointing out that although they have access in the winter for the public, for a handsome fee, that not only did participants have to be able bodied but also pretty fit and take a suitability test. I'll wait til they've all come back before I grab Ruth and suggest the sponsored swim. (See Appendix 1)

It's a couple of days later when a brief email arrives from the Olympic track at Innsbruck. I almost file it straight into the 'Charity Events' folder when I read it the first time but then I see that the answer is a 'maybe'. Innsbruck has the 'Guestbob' which is a specially adapted Bob that has one driver/brakeman at the front and then carries up to 4 passengers behind him in the Bob. It starts ¾ the way up the track as it can't quite reach the full-on speeds that the 4-man Bob can. Although they have never had a disabled person take part, technically there is no reason why. We need a couple of strong lads along to ensure we can get Ruth in and out of the Bob.

The Innsbruck 'Guestbobs'

It takes a few more email back and forth for the course director to be comfortable that we have a plan and its time to tell Ruth.

"It's all organised" I say to Ruth.

"What's organised?" she asks.

"The Bobsleigh. February 8th in the middle of the season".

"Very funny" Ruth laughs.

"No seriously, Innsbruck. They have a specially adapted Bobsleigh and they've confirmed that you can do it"

"Really?" Ruth has a great excited, yet horrified look on her face.

"Really. I know you were only kidding but they really can do it. It's the only one in the world that can mind, and we have to find at least one other person to go, but apart form that, its there if you want it".

Ruth
I'm almost speechless. My legs don't work but my mouth sure does, and often it fires off before I tell myself to shut the hell up. At this point I'm thinking that I've got myself in hot water. Within 30 seconds though I'm jumping around at the prospect. Well not literally jumping around as I'd fall out of my chair, again. What have I started here.

Steve
Over the coming weeks we identify some decent flights and book those and then enlist the help of Airmiles to find

us a hotel with decent disabled access. Then it was just a case of recruiting a couple of other people that were prepared to be thrown down a hill at 70mph+.

First to jump in is my mate Andy who has some 'previous' in that he's been involved in some fundraising escapades in the past. He's quickly followed by a colleague from work, Onno. So then there were four.

Chapter 2 – The Build Up

Steve

'Never assume' is a good phrase when it comes to planning a trip with a disabled person. It's just before Christmas and we are heading out in February and we decide to plan out the day of travel. It's an early flight so I recommend we get there a bit early, but at least we can check in online. Ruth smiles and suggests I check that – sure enough, disabled travellers can't do online check-in as they need to meet the check-in staff who double-check that the arrangements for the plane have been completed. OK, so we'll meet at the airport an extra half and hour early. Ruth smiles again, and explains that if possible, could I pick her up at her house on the way. I'd assumed she can grab the train and tube – in fact neither are wheelchair accessible.

I make a point of taking a look at the tube map and find that only a handful of the hundreds of stations have wheelchair access effectively wiping out the chance to use the tube network. Even the trains are mostly inaccessible for Ruth travelling by herself. You may think that not offering a lift straight away was heatless but Ruth knows my car – it's not the most practical. In fact, we've been down the pub several times with the roof down as quite simply it's a lot easier to get the chair in that way – sticking out of the back seats.

We take the precaution of checking that the bags and cases still fit with the wheels and chair – they do, but at a stretch. Certainly could not have had a third person in the car.

The boot of the VW is not exactly cavernous
and only just fits the main part of the chair in.

The detached wheels fit on the back seat –
nestling very tightly with the cases.

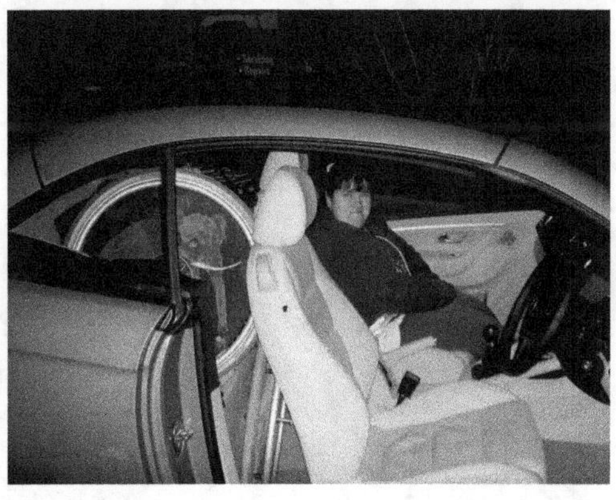

Important Tip: When considering transport for a disabled person remember they will need to go into the front seat of the car – vital if you have a very tall lad like Andy 6'5" with you – and with taxis and hire cars specify an estate as its way faster than detaching the wheels every time.

Ruth

Travelling on trains in the UK for able-bodied people is tough enough, let alone me. It sometimes appears that the staff at the majority of UK stations make it deliberately as tough as possible for someone in my situation to travel on the trains so that disabled people are discouraged from using them at all. One of the many reasons I like visiting the USA so much is that using public transport out there is less of an issue. I'm able to use the Subway, ride the Amtrak and even use most of the local and national bus companies. The UK could learn a lot from their counterparts in the US.

Chapter 3 – To the Airport

Ruth

Its getting close to the day of the trip and the weather forecast is for snow. In most countries that's not an issue but if there is more than an inch in the UK the whole country comes to a standstill. My road is very steep and there is absolutely no way Steve's going to get his car up that hill in the snow. I'm going to suggest to Steve that he picks me up late the night before and we go straight to the airport from his house.

Steve

Ruth's right. If we get caught by the snow then we are in big trouble as its an early morning flight and we have to be at the airport early so if we have to take an extra half hour to get her down her hill (what were the authorities thinking when they housed her up that hill?) in the chair and it won't be clever doing that with the temperature below freezing. I go and pick up Ruth that evening and head to mine. We encounter the first practicality of the trip. My house has no disabled loo (well think about it, how many houses are geared up for disabled access) – Ruth is confident she will be fine as she has made sure she hasn't drunk anything close to coming to our house and in an emergency we do have a downstairs loo. We get back to mine and I grab a few hours sleep while I install Ruth with a pair of wireless headphones and the Sky remote and she is well set for a night of watching movies. I hope she grabs a couple of hours of sleep.

Ruth

Steve's house is niccly laid out for a person in a wheelchair. He calls it minimalist, but I just call it tidy and uncluttered. He and Sharon have three cats and after an initial nervousness – I don't think the cats have seen a disabled person before – they seem fine with me. The largest one, Charlie, is an absolute monster, more like a small horse but dead soppy and affectionate. He's probably thinking that I am extremely friendly in that I am sitting down all the time and have my lap available permanently to jump up onto. Cats don't judge and if anything they will discriminate in favour of a disabled person as they won't get scared by sudden movements and we don't tower over them in the same way as a free standing person. I'm rambling now, probably because I've seen all the films available on the movie channels. I'm a massive movie fan and see as many films as I can when they come out at the cinema. I have an editorial card which gets me into most films either discounted or for free. I like to remind the guys at work that I actually vote for things like the Oscars. Only a few more hours to go.

Steve
The alarm wakes me at a very rude 3am and my first instinct is to check outside and although cold, there is no snow yet. That's a great sign. I get dressed and make my way downstairs. Ruth is in the middle of a movie and smiles wearily and gives a thumbs up. We sneak out the house quietly as my wife Sharon is still fast asleep upstairs. The run to the airport is a breeze at that time of the morning. Although the M25 is the most hated of all roads in the UK it means an hour to Heathrow from our place when it's the middle of the night. As we approach the M4 junction the snow starts to fall. Huge great big flakes as well.

"Do you think our flight will be ok?" asks Ruth

"We've got the best chance as ours is one of the first out" I reply. I don't want to say it but I've been stuck in many an airport in my time with Xerox and if this keeps up it's going to be touch and go.

We've reached the car park and there is now a covering of snow and its settling. I drive around for a bit until I find a disabled space that I can see will allow me to get Ruth out of the car easily. Whilst the car has very wide opening doors it can be a bit of an issue in the thinner spaces. It doesn't occur to me until I've parked up but we really need to be wary of where the bus is – I see it waiting at the end of the car park and decide to drive down and pop out and have a chat with the driver. She's really nice and offers to wait for us at the stop next to the disabled spaces so that we're not waiting in the cold too much.

Getting on the bus is very easy as there is a flap that folds down enabling me to push Ruth up into the bus. I'm about to roll Ruth in first but she points out that cases go in first, then her and vice versa on the way out. I'm learning at every step on this trip. The bus ride to the terminal is quick and Ruth is having a great time explaining to the driver, in detail, where we are off to and what we are going to be up to. I should take a picture of people's faces when she does that as there is a mixture of amazement and wonder, usually followed by "Wow, you wouldn't get me doing that".

Chapter 4 – Flight 1

Steve

Once we've rechecked everything with the main desk at the airline we head through security – there is fast track for disabled people which is a good thing as getting through the metal detectors takes a bit more time than normal. We head straight down to the gate as Ruth explains that we need to be the first on the plane. When we get to the gate Ruth talks to the ground staff and they confirm that the special chair to take Ruth on the plane has been arranged and will arrive soon.

Imagine the thinnest possible wheelchair and you have the idea – it has to be thin enough to go down the aisle in the plane. In fact you can see one in Chapter 6 as there is a photo of Ruth being lifted into the 2nd plane.

Here's where we hit the first major problem of the trip – and it's a big one. As they wheel Ruth onto the plane to her seat, which is halfway down the plane they find that the armrest is fixed on the row so Ruth can't slide into the seat. We suggest then that Ruth is moved to a row where there is a flexible armrest – the ground staff go and get the cabin crew who appear not to have hit this problem before and say that they can't change the seat allocation. When we press them they say that the only seats that are easier access are the front row which is business class and that all the seats are full. We push back and argue that it's simply not easy to get Ruth into the seat over the armrest as it's too high to get over. The plane is now beginning to fill up with annoyed passengers and a queue is building up which makes it embarrassing and frustrating as at the centre of it all is Ruth who has now been perched on the tiny chair for quite a while. The cabin crew are insisting we allow the ground staff to lift Ruth into the seat. We point out that this is going to be quite dangerous for her and we are given an ultimatum – get in the seat or get off the plane. Ruth decides that nothing is going to stop her from getting to the Bobsleigh at this late stage so she agrees to being lifted in. What follows is several minutes of awkward manoeuvring as the ground staff can't get into a position to lift properly as the seats are in the way. All the while we hear the complaints of the passengers who have been queuing in the aisle down the plane. To be fair to them can't see what's causing the hold up but it's got to be embarrassing for Ruth and I'm sure she can hear them.

Ruth is finally in her seat and in lots of discomfort as both her knee joints have been twisted quite badly in the lifting. We watch the plane fill up and the cabin crew, none of whom are smiling, go through the safety routine.

"What happens in the event of an emergency with you" I ask Ruth.

"I stay on the plane" she says simply.

"Its one thing you take for granted if you travel on a plane as a disabled person. If the worst happens then you will be left there – which is fair enough."

I can't believe how calmly she says that. My brain starts to rattle into what could in fact be done for a disabled person in an emergency and begin to come to the same conclusions. If it took them five minutes to lift Ruth in with a couple of meaty ground crew lads to help her, then when everyone is clambering to get out of a burning plane Ruth is probably right, there isn't going to be much of a chance to help. Doesn't feel right but before I can get too wound up about it Ruth pipes up. "At least we have breakfast to look forward to" she smiles.

The plane takes off and we are underway. We can see the cabin crew head our way and after a few minutes the lady asks what we would like to drink. I have an orange juice, a water and a coffee but Ruth doesn't fancy anything. We get given our breakfast and Ruth reminds the lady that she is vegetarian.

"We stopped the vegetarian meals a few months ago" replies the lady.

"That's ok" Ruth says, "Whatever you have that doesn't have meat in". For the first time I hear a little resignation in Ruth's voice.

"I'm sorry but this is all we have. We can take the meat out of the sandwich for you" comes the offer.

Ruth politely declines. I'm about to kick off about it but I can see it won't do any good. We both sit back and let the flight go by – neither of us is in the mood for talking.

> *Important Tip: Always have some backup food with you in the case of travelling with a vegetarian. A banana or a chocolate bar in the bag would have gone down a treat at that moment.*

Ruth
I'm really p****** off with this situation. We had made our travel plans well in advance and let the airline know

that I would need assistance to the plane and an accessible seat. Their system should automatically know which armrests move and which don't. This had all been agreed but being crammed and bashed into a seat was certainly not what I requested. The fact is the ground crew aren't listening to me when I try to explain that bending my legs in weird angles wouldn't help and that they were hurting me. It's amazing how many people assume that because I don't have movement in my legs means I can't feel them – I bloody well can. In fact, it never ceases to amaze me how many people think that because I am in a wheelchair I am also mentally disabled. If I had a pound for every time someone has talked to me like a small child from the off then I'd be a rich girl. Anyway, after this hassle I really could do with something to eat. A warm snack would help my muscles which are beginning to tense up. But apparently if I wanted my vegetarian meal I needed to fly a couple of months ago. I suppose I could risk a coffee as it's a very short flight but I'm not tempting fate, and besides I don't want to talk to the flight attendants (who look like the Stepford Wives) and explain that they may need to help me to the bathroom. So I think I'll sit here with a frozen smile for this part of the trip.

Notes: Austrian Airlines and Airmiles

At this point we'd like to send a big thank you out to Austrian Airlines and Airmiles. Whilst the process broke down this time on the plane, the airline and agents responded very well to our feedback. After our trip we wrote to them both and they immediately launched internal investigations and took on the task of ensuring the processes were tightened to ensure that the same issues don't happen again.

Both Ruth and I are practical enough to know that every eventuality can't be avoided. How organisations react to problems, and importantly the manner in which they do it makes the difference.

The teams within Airmiles and Austrian both handled the issue with professionalism and tact and between them they came back with fair answers and some help towards our next trip.

In going through the process Ruth shared with me issues that she has had when travelling by air. Many times she has been left on the plane while the staff clean the plane around her because someone has forgotten to organise the chair to take her off the plane. She has often been made to feel that somehow its 'her fault' , and that she is the one to blame for having to run a different process.

Some airlines seem to try and discourage disabled people from travelling with them by introducing excessive extra charges for handling the wheelchairs. In the last section of the book you will read about one exciting disabled entrepreneur that has set up a travel company dedicated to organising trips for sight impaired travellers. Not only is it an inspiring idea, but one founded in good business sense. There are several million disabled people in the UK, and if you include the elderly infirm that share some similar mobility issues, then you have a very large potential market. Ever hear of the Grey Pound? Well there is a big and strong slice of that which has a tough time moving around.

Providing hassle-free travel options for this sector should be something the travel companies take more seriously than they do. After all, you can tailor your travel options based on cuisine easy enough – with options from vegetarian through to Halal meal options but we are yet to see any travel companies that are taking the needs of the disabled community seriously.

The market is about to get significantly bigger as well. The new parts of the tube network are all wheelchair accessible – so what will happen to the market when the Docklands Light Railway (DLR) extension is complete and disabled travellers can get on a train straight into London City Airport? Terminal 5 at Heathrow is another big opportunity. The strategy teams within the short haul airlines should be planning their play for this new market.

Some long haul carriers like American Airlines (AA) have been ahead of the curve for some years, perhaps as Ruth mentioned before due to the progressive attitude to disabled travel in the USA. Ruth raves about how she is treated on AA and won't entertain going with anyone else on her annual trips to the states. They have a customer for life there.

Now I can almost hear the more negative among you thinking that the only reason the US market is ahead of the UK is the litigious nature of the country – i.e. if companies don't meet the legislation someone will undoubtedly sue them, so they meet the legislation. Well, I can't totally dismiss that argument, but whatever is causing it, in the end those service providers that make themselves 'disabled accessible' often find that the benefits in incremental business outweigh the costs of implementation.

Chapter 5 – Vienna Airport

Steve

So. We've made it into Vienna airport. It's not bad as airports go. We've a few hours in between flights so time enough for lunch but first stop is loo break. It's pretty bloody obvious when you think about it but Ruth hasn't had a chance to go since we left the main area in Heathrow. I feel a bit bad about not realising but as she explained while we work our way through the airport, there is no chance for her to go on the plane so she daren't have anything to drink on the plane either – so it's pretty important to find a loo then get a drink as she's dehydrated from the flight. There I was with my water and a tea on the flight and didn't think when she decided to have nothing on the plane. Am beginning to get a crash course in the practicalities for disabled people travelling.

> *Important Tip: hand luggage for the helper – you can't go wrong with a back-pack. You will, at many times need both hands to push the chair and within a few minutes any weight split across your arms will be uncomfortable. The back-pack is a lifesaver.*

We reach the first disabled loo and Ruth comes straight back out and asks if I don't mind if we find another one. I'm not about to make joke this time but Ruth must have seen it in my face that I'm wondering why, so she explains.

"This disabled toilet has been fitted by a sub-contractor – you can tell. Whereas all the pieces have been fitted properly, they are in the wrong place. In particular the height of the seat is above the normal toilet height – too high for a disabled person to get across easily. If there's no alternative then you have to manage somehow – but let's check a couple of the other ones".

Fortunately the next one has been fitted properly. Ruth goes on to explain that many a fall out of her wheelchair has been prompted by a badly fitted toilet. That's one place in the world you don't want to be falling out of your chair.

Ruth
What I find with so many public toilets for the disabled is that the rails and hand bars have been put in, but in all the wrong places – or that there are so many that they end up getting in the way. An even worse design is as in this case where the toilet has been fitted higher than my wheelchair and it's almost impossible to transfer over.

Steve
I let Ruth choose lunch. Italian, local food or burgers. We end up at Hagen Daas. Ruth tells me that I can classify the lunch as salad with a dressing – ice cream with chocolate sauce on top - works for me. We take up a couple of small round tables in the restaurant. Lunch is great – nothing beats ice cream. Ruth is really animated about the Bobsleigh – she's so excited. We steam through the ice cream and decide to explore the airport shops to see what they have to offer.

Salad Ruth style – with 'chocolate' dressing

Due to the route out of the restaurant – navigating our way through the tables I load up with all the bags (looking like a Christmas tree) and leave Ruth to wheel herself and follow me out.

She shouts after me,

"So you're not going to give me a push then". I turn around, slowly to make sure I don't knock into the tables with the bags. I smile and reply in a mock harsh tone,

"I'll give you a push if you really want". Ruth does her best 'shocked' face and replies in a sheepish tone.

"Oh please don't push me down the stairs again, it really hurt last time".

This puts a big grin on my face until I turn back around to see a sea of faces looking at me as if I was pure evil. As we walk out past the angry faces and shaking heads I make a note to explain to Ruth (which she finds hilarious) that Austrian's generally don't do sarcasm.

Till the day I die I won't forget the look on the lady behind the counter. I don't think I could have got a more shocked reaction if I had shot a puppy in front of them.

Ruth

Have you ever seen the movie 'Ghost' when Patrick Swayze's character and his friend are in the elevator. They start talking in load voices about how they had been to the doctor to get rid of contagious rash. My friend Kris and I have our own version of that scene when we are waiting for the lift and Kris' pretends to get impatient and she starts pushing me towards the door for the stairs. I pipe up saying "Please Kris, I'll be good, don't push me down the stairs again".

I guess it was the sugar rush from the ice cream that made me re-enact the scene with Steve. Judging by the look on his face though, perhaps I should have warned him about it beforehand.

Chapter 6 – Flight 2

Steve

Unlike the first plane, which has a walkway to it and is what you would describe as a normal sized plane, this one, apparently is a 'toy' one. Innsbruck, we are told by the nice airline lady, is in the middle of the mountains so getting in there with a little plane is a might easier.

So it's out onto the runway for this one. Ruth is pretty impressed that we get our own bus just for the two of us.

Vienna – Ruth's Bus

The staff are very attentive and nothing is too much trouble for them. The bus arrives in plenty of time and takes us out to the plane. Its been a while since I've been on one this small and Ruth and I amuse ourselves by asking the cabin staff where they have to wind it up to get it going (they are not biting however). Access to the seats is very easy on this one as all of the armrests lift up. We do encounter the same challenge with the temporary chair as we did on the previous flight though. Everyone wants to help, but the easiest thing is for Ruth to lift herself across.

> *Important Tip: Most disabled people in a chair develop strong upper body strength and are expert at how to move themselves in and out of their chair. 'Helping' them move can often actually be a hindrance so always ask first.*

Lifting the temporary chair into the plane

When we get to Innsbruck airport, after a very nerve racking descent in amongst the mountains, we stop to marvel at the surrounding mountains. The town has snow capped mountains all around it and from the moment you land to the moment you leave they dominate the skyline. Definitely a place to take the camera and the constant presence of the mountains helps build the anticipation that within a few hours we will be hurtling down the mountain in an oversized tin can.

Mountains, mountains everywhere.

Ruth

It may be a smaller plane but it's far more comfortable as I have the leg room I need and I am able to stretch out and take the pressure off my knees. My legs are very sore but not enough to distract me from the adventure that is only a few hours away. I'd been to Innsbruck many years before and it feels good to be back. The cabin crew on this flight are much more friendly and didn't make me feel like I shouldn't be there. I feel more relaxed and am going to try and grab a quick nap.

Chapter 7 – Up The Hill

Steve
We're due to meet the lads at the hotel so it's a quick pickup of the hire car (note – prepare yourself for a price-shock with hire cars in Innsbruck, the additional supplements like 'winter tyres' are high) which is a decent sized estate car and we are off to the hotel. It's not too hard to find and we check in. The hotel has organised Ruth a disabled access room on the ground floor and we meet up with the lads in the hotel lobby and it's off to the track. We have loads of time to spare as we need to be there at 6pm to get ready to go up the hill.

The first thing you see once you've parked up and walk to the gatehouse is the 'finish' line which in fact you end up going through upwards as the Bob has to go uphill at the end to slow it down.

The track looks daunting when you see the height of the corners. Then something flies down past you and you start to wonder whether it's such a good idea after all.

There is a nice café at the bottom and we decide that a beer for the lads (coffee for Onno the driver) is the perfect thing to settle the uneasy stomachs.

We strike up a conversation with one of the staff and the competitive side comes out as we ask how long it takes to get from the top to the bottom.

"It takes from 47 to 49 seconds to complete the run".

"What makes the difference, in other words how can we make it go faster?" asks Onno.

"It depends on the weight" he replies.

"The heavier the passengers, the faster it goes". He takes a long look at our group, lingering on the man mountain that is Andy.

"For you 47 seconds" he adds without even the hint of a smile. I open my mouth but Andy gives me a clip on the head before I get a chance to add anything.

All around the walls are some wonderful pictures of the track. We're all getting really excited now. We check the watches and decide its time to get to the bottom of the hill where we will be picked up to go to the top.

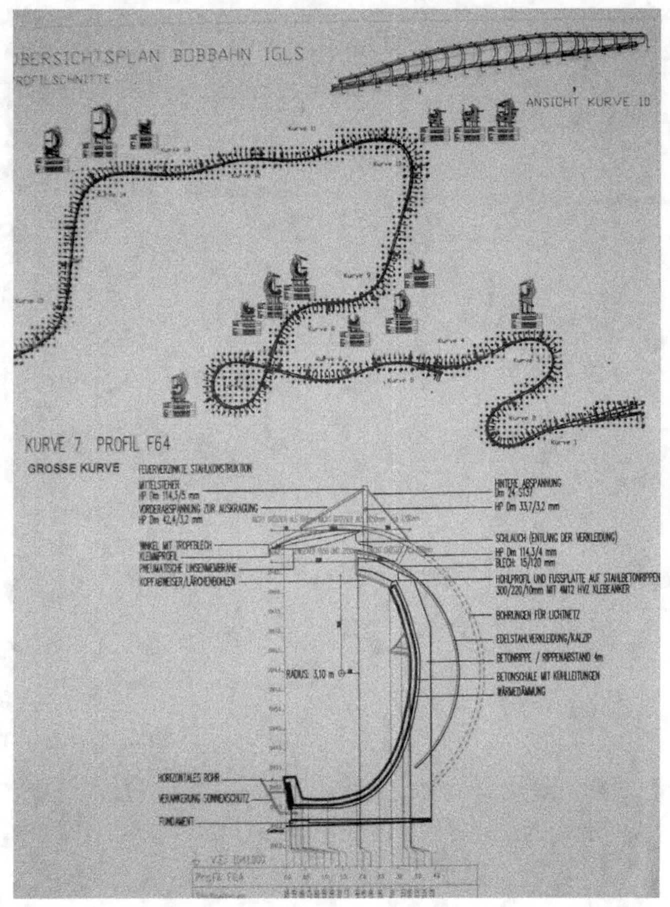

The bottom diagram shows the steepness of the turns.

Aerial Photograph of the twisting Bobsleigh Track

We make our way to the bottom of the track where the truck will meet us to take us to the top. While we are waiting several two man Bobs and even some luges come flying down the track.

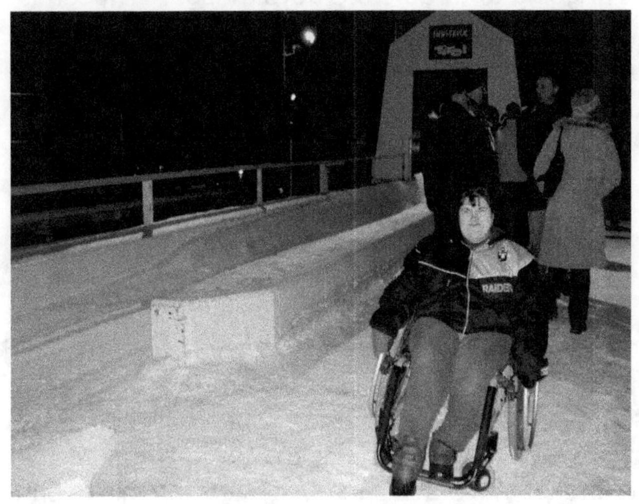

While you wait your adrenalin is fuelled by the
Bobs coming to their finish behind a small wall of ice.

We realise we've made another mistake here. The wait is quite a long one and the temperature has now dropped well below zero. Whilst the boys stamp up and down and can keep their circulation going, Ruth is getting colder and colder.

Ruth
To put it mildly my circulation is crap at the best of times. I'm the girl that has icy legs in the middle of a Californian heat-wave. This is a first for me. I've not been on a

mountain at this time of night before. When I was skiing in competition it was always in the morning or during the day when the temperature is higher. This is the reverse the temperature is getting colder and colder and I'm turning into the tin man from the Wizard of Oz. There's no way I'm going to trouble the guys though, I'll laugh it out.

Important Tip: Temperature regulation may be an issue for a disabled person. Especially important in extremely cold conditions make sure you have made provision to keep warm.

Steve
The truck arrives and we literally have to climb in the open backed truck. They use the same truck to take the Bobs back up the hill – by sliding them into the back. This presents us with an amusing but challenging way of keeping Ruth from falling out the back. Not sure that the chairs brakes have been stress tested for this eventuality we are all laughing as the truck ambles up the snow-covered road bouncing around with each of the three boys holding onto the side with one hand and the chair with the other.

We get to the top and there is a massive group of people. We try and talk to the guys at the top and explain that we have permission from the track manager but despite Onno's half decent command of the German language we are struggling. They finally agree that once the rest of the people have gone down we can go in the last Bob. Another mistake. We wait about twenty minutes for the last of the group to head down four at a time and it's finally your turn. We're a few metres away from the goal.

As we go to lift Ruth out of her chair she moves to lift herself up and cries out in pain.

"Ahhhh. My knee's gone. It's come out". We tell the staff to back off and Ruth explains through a wall of tears that her knee has dislocated. I immediately wince as having dislocated my shoulder years before I know how painful it is.

"I can't go down" Ruth cries. "I can't do it". Andy and I look at each other and out first instinct is to get Ruth into the warm. There is a command cabin up there and we wheel Ruth in.

"OK. One of us will stay here with you and the other two will get the truck down to the car and come back up and get you" Onno says.

"Oh no you don't" says Ruth. "I'm not ruining this for you. You're going down. I'll be fine here".

No matter how much we argue Ruth is insistent and the three boys don helmets and clamber into the Bob.

Ruth
I've come so close to achieve something I've always wanted to do and my body's beaten me again. The events of the day have basically come together to beat my weak, crap legs. Being manhandled on the plane and the stress around that and then waiting in the cold has drained me. What I think finally caused my knee to go out was the truck ride to the top of the hill. The guys were holding the chair but I was having to brace myself too to stop falling out. My right leg is longer than my left so all the bumps and pressure were going on that keen all the way to the

top of the run. Once at the top there is another bit of waiting around. Finally it's our turn to go down and I move forward in my seat and the knee just pops out. The pain is incredible and I know instantly that I can't go into the Bobsleigh. The emotions are hard to describe. Despite being in terrible pain my tears are for the disappointment of having come this far.

I insist that everyone else goes down – they argue but there's no way I'm ruining it for them. Steve knows how stubborn I am so he gives in and they head off in the Bob. While I am waiting for them in the warm hut I find myself telling myself off for letting the pain get to me and telling off my knee for not staying in its socket until after the run.

The start of the Bobsleigh is at the top of a small slope that feeds into the main track.

Steve
We all feel awful as we climb into the Bobsleigh. This trip was all about Ruth and here we are leaving her at the top of the hill. Refusing to do the ride would just have made Ruth feel worse though. The ride itself is incredible. It starts with a mild straight bit and a very light turn mid way through which gives you a false 'it's not that scary after all' feeling. Then it hits the first bend and you realise that any rollercoaster you've been on before isn't a path on this. Your stomach feels like it's in your throat and the speed is intense.

As the turns hit you, you find yourself pausing for breath on the all but brief straight bits. Although the total ride time is just that 47 seconds it feels like several minutes as the walls of ice fly by, seemingly right by the sides of your face.

As the Bob comes to a stop we clamber out and all of our legs have turned to jelly. As we come down from the adrenalin high we straight away head to the car and drive up to collect Ruth.

The car is not a great place to be as we head back to the hotel. There is plenty of bravado about coming back next year but underlying there is frustration and disappointment in all our voices. We end up with the last ten minutes very quiet and we agree to meet up in the lobby in half an hour to head into town for a bite to eat and to drown our sorrows.

Ruth
I feel horrible in the car back to Innsbruck. Onno asks if I want to see a doctor. I say no. I know my body better than most doctors, after all, this bloody knee has

dislocated before. Often doctors make it worse when they try and help. I call Mum and Dad and Linda to let them know things haven't gone to plan. All I want to do is cry again when I hear their voices. I feel horrible like I've let everyone down. I have to find a way of making things right.

Nothing like a ½ metre beer to get over a Bobsleigh.
'Got to have one of those' says Onno.

Steve

Within five minutes of arriving at the restaurant Ruth is already talking about the details of the next trip.

"We can take the same hotel. It's not perfect, but not bad at all."

I know she's hurting inside and we spend most of the evening talking about the next trip. I have to admit that the boys are great. They treat Ruth as one of the lads and she loves that. If you think too much about what to say and how to behave in that kind of situation and it's almost harder to find the right things to say. We joke about all the normal things and Ruth shares another little gem that she is the ideal travelling partner for women as she is at exactly the right height to check out the local talent's bums.

"I've got a few of my friends that would really like to meet you then Ruth" jokes Andy.

Ruth has the most amazing stories from her sporting past, most of which can't be written down in a book, but I wanted to share one with you that literally made the guys weep with laughter in the restaurant (lubricated with beer of course). Ruth had been competing with a disabled team and was staying with the team in a nice hotel somewhere in the UK. She explained that the disabled teams tended to be quite lively and that light drinking wasn't the norm (we're going back a few years here so the strict health and diet regimes of the last decade hadn't arrived yet). One of the athletes had a reputation for practical jokes – itching powder in false limb joints, loosening wheelchair bolts and the like. Well, on this particular night the practical joker, who happened to be a double amputee, had drunk one too many beers and had passed out and her team mates decided it was payback time and decided to hide her legs.

Ruth, with a huge grin, went on to explain that the problem came the next morning when, nursing some monster hangovers, none of the team could remember where they stashed the legs. What followed you couldn't include in any kind of comedy show – well one that could ever be shown for political correctness reasons. A complete team of disabled athletes and every member of hotel staff turning the place upside down looking for a pair of legs. Apparently they found them about an hour later nestling at the back of a storage cupboard.

The staff in the restaurant have also warmed to Ruth and her boundless energy and we have a regular stream of the waiters and waitresses coming to check on us and cracking jokes with our table. Several ½ metre beers are consumed – and many cokes for Ruth. Despite indulgence in the past Ruth is now a strict teetotal. A pledge she made several years ago to show solidarity with a close friend and she sticks to it religiously. More to admire, considering her exploits include her being fished out of the Hemel Hempstead canal on several occasions when she had been drunk in charge of her chair.

We all have a great meal and squeeze in a couple of beers back at the hotel while Ruth calls it a night. The boys have really taken to Ruth and the bravado to come back next year is strong. We head back to the room (we'd gone with a triple on account of cost) and within minutes of our heads hitting the pillows Onno is sorely regretting ignoring my advice to bring ear plugs as Andy's snoring reaches its usual 'warthog being strangled' level.

Chapter 8 – Innsbruck

Triangulation

Important Tip: When you are going shopping with a disabled person, first stop is to find a good, clean, working disabled toilet and use that place as a triangulation point. It saves a lot of time later.

The Schwarofsky Gallery

Excellent collection of Schwarofsky ornaments – really special and the pictures can't do them justice. Add to that "one of the best" disabled toilets Ruth has seen and you have a five star rating on our trip. Hats off to the staff too as they seem to be as welcoming the fourth time we visit as they did the first time.

Stunning displays, easy access and good facilities. Five stars for the gallery.

Fish and surgery for lunch

So its time for lunch and the small streets of Innsbruck yield plenty of nice looking cafes and restaurants but we pick one that's on the main street as Ruth fancies some fish and from a practical point of view we can see daylight between the rows of tables and it looks like we can get in and move around without too much hassle.

Lunch is delicious – some sort of grilled fish with a very nice sauce. Despite the events of the previous day Ruth is incredibly up-beat and already talking about the fact that this way round she gets two shopping trips in Innsbruck. Disaster strikes at the end of the meal when, having eaten a bit much I sit back and cross my feet and in the process manage to catch Ruth's dislocated knee. After a huge scream in pain, which scares the **** out of me. I don't know what to do as Ruth is grimacing in pain – I mean, what is the usual thing to do when you've kicked a disabled person in their dislocated knee?

An uncomfortable minute goes by as I say 'sorry' repeatedly. Ruth wipes away the tears, her eyes have watered as she has teeth clenched through the pain, and begins to laugh.

"Thanks Steve" she said and before I can apologise again she adds. "No really, thanks. How you did it I don't know but you've managed to kick my knee back into place. The chances of you doing that are tiny – just promise me you'll never do it again!".

The Davidoff Bar

After checking out a bunch of easily accessible shops (not bad here, but once again its something you don't think of when you go shopping) we head back to the cigar bar that we saw on the way into the centre. When we get to the front of the bar we see the front door that we didn't realise from the other side of the road. Five nice big steps down to the bar's very elegant glass fronted façade. We look at the steps and at each other and are both probably thinking what a shame we won't get a cigar when the manageress comes out. A very elegantly dressed lady who says hello and pauses as she's thinking of how to say what she is thinking in German, in English.

"The lady cannot walk?" she asked finally.
Whilst I can think of a few smart answers, and I'm sure Ruth has some choice comments too we can both see the question is quite genuine.

"No. The lady cannot walk" I reply simply.

"Perhaps I may have a solution" replies the lady and comes up to meet us at the top of the stairs. She leads us to the side of the building where the entrance to the kitchen is a slow ramp down which the barrels and drinks cages are lined up.

"Would it be ok to come into the kitchen?" she asks.
I take a quick look at Ruth who is grinning so I take that as a yes. We proceed to enter the exclusive surroundings of the cigar bar with its wonderful interior and even more wonderful cigar smell across the wet kitchen tiles and past the bins.

Once inside the bar is really nice. Suffice to say we make a slightly odd party in the large bar – we are surrounded by ample-bellied businessmen and the odd pretty 'pa' or 'niece'. It seems that brandy is pretty compulsory here too so I decide, when in Rome. We select a size of cigar that while we have a chance of finishing them before the end of the day, it will be a stretch. There aren't many more relaxing things than a glass of good (if expensive) brandy and a good cigar. I have to admit its one of the larger cigar's I've smoked and it takes a bit over an hour which gives us plenty of time to gossip away.

Ruth

I could tell straight away that the manageress was being genuine and not patronising in her approach. You get used to the signs. As I don't drink I was very boring once she had settled us in our area and had a coke. The lady made our hour there very pleasant as she came over from time to time to make sure that everything was ok while Steve and I put the world to rights. While we are enjoying the atmosphere I'm able to stretch my legs. The pain in my right knee is beginning to subside. It's a relief that it's back in place despite the fact that it took a kick to get I there.

Architecture in Innsbruck is worth a trip in itself

Homage to South Park

Andy's headed home and Onno has spent the day snowboarding with his super-fast sharpened racing snowboard (nutter) and has arranged to meet us in town for dinner. The centre of Innsbruck is really nicely lit up in the evening and it's a pleasant walk across from the bar where we have agreed to meet Onno and the main central area where we will find a restaurant. As we cross the tram lines Ruth starts laughing that if we were truly cruel we could wedge her wheels in the tracks and wait for the next tram "Would make an excellent video for You Tube" she says. We decide instead to pay homage to South Park (we are all fans)[Kenny]. Makes us laugh every time we see the picture.

[Kenny] For the uninitiated in most episodes of South Park the character 'Kenny' is killed off in a variety of grisly ways, always greeted by the reaction "Oh my god, they've killed Kenny – you bastards".

The Thai Restaurant

Walking and wheeling around the centre of Innsbruck you can see what wonderful architecture the town has. We're not in any hurry to fund somewhere to eat so we take in the sights and the buildings and peer through the windows of several restaurants before we settle upon a very nice looking Thai restaurant as all three of us fancy something interesting and spicy.

We take a table for four and the staff are very accommodating not making too much of a fuss but efficiently ensure that we can get an easy access table.

We get the drinks in and as usual Ruth is on the Coke while Onno and I go for the Thai beer. We're checking through the menus and order – a variety of Thai curries times for the boys and Ruth goes for some sort of noodle dish. The waiter collects the menus and the drinks arrive.

"So Ruth, how come your legs don't work" asks Onno. Right off the bat, first question. I'm about to remind Ruth that Onno's Dutch and that is a characteristic of the Dutch culture to be direct but she smiles and responds matter of factly.

"I was born with no movement in my legs. I have feeling in them, but I can't move them".

"Ok" shrugs Onno and the conversation switches to the quality of the snow for the snowboarding that day.

While Onno and Ruth have an animated discussion about whether skiing or snowboarding is the best I reflect that I have known Ruth for many years and had never asked the reason she was in a wheelchair. Is it the reserved nature of British that leads us to avoid such questions. I must admit I feel a little stupid. To Onno it was an obvious question, one that would avoid misunderstanding and complications later on. To Ruth it's a simple fact that, talking to her about it later, is one that she prefers not to avoid. Being open and frank about it is not an issue.

"So which events did you take part in on your sit-ski?" Onno asks.

"Pretty much all of them." Ruth answers. "Slalom, Super-G, downhill. You can get some serious speed up on a sit-ski". She laughs.

"Wait a minute" I say. "You must be fearless or mad to fly downhill on a sit-ski. I saw the downhill track at Val D'Isere and I wouldn't be able to go down it on my skis slowly unless there was fresh snow".

"Yep. That one's pretty steep" Ruth admits. "But there are lots worse. The other problem is the extra weight you have with the sit-ski is that if you catch the safety barriers at the wrong angle you can make it through. One time I lost it on the downhill and broke through the barrier. Luckily about a second after I went through I hit a very big rock which stopped me a few metres from the edge".

"From the edge of what?" Onno asks.

"Oh there was a cliff there". Ruth shrugs.

Onno and I look at each other shaking our heads and smiling. Fearless.

"So, you get to similar speeds as the standard skiers?" Onno asks.

"Well, nearly except we have a higher wind resistance so they can get a bit quicker. But we always beat them at tree-skiing".

"Tree skiing?" I ask

"Yes – off-piste through the trees" Onno adds. He's a seriously good skier as well as snowboarder and has done his fair share of off-piste.

"Yes. We're faster as we can avoid the lower branches as we can get under them whereas the standard skiers have to avoid them which slows them down". Ruth adds.

The more I hear the more I can see that the intensity with which Ruth has applied herself to everything she has taken on. I'm not a bad skier but stay away from off-piste and there she was racing able-bodied skiers, of national standard, through the trees.

The food arrives and it's excellent. We have some fun with the waiter when Ruth decides that nothing grabs her fancy on the dessert menu except the pretty looking Dragon fruit which is part of the menu design.

"Can we have one of those" she says. "I'll ask. I had one a few months ago, they are about the size of a lemon" I add. Onno laughs. "You can try" he says " but you may have a challenge". The waiter heads to the kitchen and when he comes back he offers a compromise of a half to share between us as they only have one left and they use is as an ingredient. When it turns up I can see why he was so perplexed as the half is the size of a melon. Onno smiles.

"I wondered if it would be that big. We came across them in Vietnam when we went travelling. They were that big there too." I'm pleasantly surprised as the fruit is lovely and sweet and finishes the meal off perfectly. The one I had from a supermarket in the UK was quite bland and small. Lesson learnt.

Cost-Saving

As we wheel down into the underground car-park, through the car entrance as we can't find the lifts, we uncover a very nice little cost saving tip. As Ruth whizzes towards the barrier she finds that it rises up. This presents us with a new parking ticket which is much cheaper to validate than the one in Onno's pocket. Ruth reveals that this is a well-known trick but not all sensors will trigger with the weight/wheel combination. Her advice, don't take a chance with a skinny disabled friend as it may not work.

Important Tip: Choose a heavy set disabled person if you are planning on 'car park ticket discounting'.

The snow capped mountains make a wonderful
backdrop to Innsbruck, especially at night

Chapter 9 – Last Minute Checks

Steve
We're getting really excited now with only a month to go. I'm finishing a few days early for Christmas so have only a few more days in the office to finalise the last few things with Ruth. Double-checked with the hotel and that's all sorted. Andy will join us – Onno can't get any decent flights so it will be the three of us. One of the key things to get done is Ruth's check with her specialist.

The re-check with the specialist is really important as Ruth has seen a deterioration in her condition over the last twelve months. What brought it home to her was her recent visit to the US. Every year Ruth uses most of her holidays to take a long trip to the US to visit friends. Considering the hassle that travelling causes, taking a three week break is a good idea. What Ruth found was that this trip in November was the toughest one she has had and that some of the basics that didn't cause an issue before are now becoming struggle.

I'm actually walking around Homebase to get some light bulbs when my mobile goes and it's Ruth. I can tell straight away that something's not right by the way she says who it is.

"We can't do the bobsleigh" she says. "The specialist says that if I do it there is more than a 50% chance I could shatter my pelvis. I'm so sorry about this, it's like my damn body is beating me again."

I'm not sure what to say. "Well we'll just have to find something else to do" is all I can muster.

"He says that it's a good thing that we didn't do it last time as there would have been a chance back then too of damage to my pelvis" Ruth adds. "It's not fair that you've done all this preparation, what with the flights and hotels and cars and everything".

"Ah that's not important – what is important is that we found out in time before we did something stupid. The main thing is what can we find you that's just as fast and scary – we need to find something that will scare the **** out of you just as much". This gets a laugh and I can hear a glimmer of the old Ruth. "What about a car, can we do a car?"

"Yes, they said a car is ok it's just the juddering of the bobsleigh with the weakness of my bones, they wouldn't be able to cope. Maybe we can get Lewis Hamilton to drive me around the track?" Ruth laughs.

"OK, well, perhaps we might not get Lewis himself to be able to drive. I know there are some tracks that do fast driving like Ferraris".

"Oh no, you can't do Ferrari's" Ruth adds in a mock serious tone "Lewis would never allow that. It's his deadly rivals, you can't do Ferrari".

"Ok. So that's what we'll do. Tomorrow I will get in touch with the race tracks and see what we can do – and no Ferraris".

We say our goodbyes and I hang up the mobile. I have to stop and take a few deep breaths. I can't believe we were so close to risking Ruth's health. Thank god we checked again and this time with the specialist.

A shudder runs through my spine as I think of what might have happened last time too. What a bizarre twist of fate that Ruth's knee dislocated. I can't imagine what would have happened if she has been injured. I try not to think of what could have happened and concentrate on turning the situation around.

I don't get much sleep that night as the thought of ruining someone's life by not checking thoroughly enough keeps running through my brain.

Ruth
I've always pushed myself to the absolute limit in everything that I do, and despite the new limitations I find myself up against, I'm determined that that isn't going to change. I feel absolutely gutted when I find out that for all the effort the Bobsleigh just isn't going to happen. If I go ahead with it and the worst does happen then I could be left not being able to do anything. It goes against the grain for me to have to say no to something, to not follow through and achieve the goal I have set myself. On this occasion I simply have to. My friends and family who have helped raise money for Leonard Cheshire are all saying that it doesn't matter, they know I tried – and I did make sure the boys went down the hill. But I need to feel that they didn't sponsor me for nothing.

The idea of a high speed drive could be the perfect solution. When I had the conversation with the specialist and the Doctor they didn't rule that out but Steve's right when he says that this time we need to leave nothing to chance and get a letter from them to confirm that they are ok with me doing it. Only one condition, no Ferrari's – over my dead body.

Chapter 10 – Fighting Back

Steve

In sorting out the details with Leonard Cheshire I decide to do some more background reading on Ruth's previous exploits as I wanted to capture how Ruth manages to bounce back time after time. I manage to get hold of a great article from YAP magazine (for Parkinsons' sufferers) which is an interview with Ruth from a couple of years ago. It's a fascinating insight into the steel and determination that runs through Ruth, and indeed many disabled people. I'll let Ruth's words take it from here.

Extract from YAP Magazine:

"People often ask me if there were a cure for my disability tomorrow, would I take it. My answer would be no, and now I'm going to tell you why. I was born with my disability – Athrogryposis – which affects my joints, muscles and nerve endings, and in a lot of ways is very similar to Polio. If affects a few people around the world and its typical of me to get something unusual – I always have to be different from everyone else. It was tough on my Mum and Dad having their first child born with a disability. They wondered if they'd somehow done something wrong and had somehow caused it. But it was simply a fluke of nature. It was awful for them too when they had to give me my physical therapy as I used to scream from the pain of having to have my joints manipulated to give them some flexibility. My Granny Gurney used to leave the room when it was being done as it used to upset her too much. I was in and out of hospital a lot when I was growing up. When I was ten, I was in hospital for different surgeries for an entire year. Mum and Dad were terrific as they juggled trips to Great Ormond

Street hospital to see me and give equal time to Sarah, my sister. Dad who's a vicar was also busy giving needed time to his parish. Being in and out of hospital caused some delays in my education. I started senior school (I attended a regular comprehensive) a year later than my fellow students and this set me apart along with my disability in their eyes. I had a pretty rotten time at school with bullies and I was pleased when I could leave. But I stuck it out, not even telling my parents that I was being bullied, as I didn't want them to worry.

Something that helped me through my school years was my involvement in the British sports association for the disabled BSAD, which is now known as Disability Sport England (DSE). I'd always ridden horses from and early age, breaking my collarbone show jumping in a competition at one stage. The horse I was riding decided he didn't like the fence and stopped suddenly. When I ride I do it all by balance as my legs don't grip. You can probably guess what happened – the horse stopped but I didn't. I went straight over his head and landed the other side of the fence breaking my collar bone.

Through DSE I got to national and international level in swimming, athletics and skiing. I particularly enjoyed the skiing as I've always been a bit of a crazy girl and a daredevil. I think that first started when I got Sarah to drag me up the stairs on the end of a skipping rope so that I could figure out a way of getting up the stairs without having to get Mum and Dad to help me. The only downside in my sporting career was that I never made it to the Paralympics because of some of the rules and regulations. The swimming and the skiing were the sports I was best at. In the swimming one of the rules was that you had to be able to swim at least two strokes. With my disability I have problems swimming on my front as I can't turn my neck enough to take a breath. I am very fast on my back though, just as fast as someone on their front. So really there shouldn't have been a problem. Backstroke in Backstroke and Backstroke in Freestyle. Why call it Freestyle if you can't choose the stroke that you want to swim? In the skiing I had a similar problem in that I was told that I had to use a particular type of sit-ski by the International Olympic Committee (IOC). Unfortunately though I couldn't manage to use this one because I've got what I describe as back to front hands that I can't straighten.

Ruth in Chiesa in 1990 on her sit-ski

Although I never made it to the Paralympics, I know I gave it my all and was good enough to represent my country in other competitions. With skiing I could also beat able-bodied skiers which is some accomplishment on its own I think. And I feel that I proved if you're determined enough and prepared to take the bad with the good that anything is possible. I retired from competitive sport a few years ago now, but I still swim to keep in shape and I've still got my medals and trophies that I won and I have kept in touch with many of my friends from my competition days.

Ruth in Tignes in 1991

Better than winning trophies and medals though for me are the friendships I've made not just through my sports but through my life in general. Three of my closest friends are Cheryl, Pam and Linda.

Cheryl and I did get to know each other through sport. She used to be a competitive ice dancer, which is one of my favourite sports although I've never been able to stand up on ice skates myself, but not through lack of trying. Like me she retired from competition a few years ago but now she teaches and trains the up and coming skaters in the West Midlands area.

The closest I get to doing my version of Torvill and Dean (apart from when I fall out of my wheelchair) is when I'm dancing with Pam. We both love going to a party together and taking over the dance floor. I'm far more dangerous than Pam as I'm doing wheelies and I usually run over your toes if you're in my way.

Linda and I, who I met through a mutual friend, hit it off immediately. I think because we both have had to go through some tough times in our lives. I have a great deal of respect for Linda who is just as determined as I am. When I'm having a bad day I often say to myself "Linda wouldn't give up even though she might want to.. I mustn't give up either". Linda is about the only person who gets away with telling me what to do. I've got a really stubborn streak in me.

Looking towards the future, something I would really love to do is go and live and work in America. I was a civil servant for the Department of Work and Pensions for ten years, but two years ago I left to train as an editor for film and television, something I've always had a fascination in. There is something very satisfying I find with editing in that you can take the raw footage and put your own feel on the material by piecing the story together, like an artist with a painting.

I had a big setback when the person who said he was going to sponsor me with training and future turned out to be not such a nice guy and let me down badly. The guy was arrested for fraud and imprisoned for lots of business deals that weren't on the level. I was made to look pretty foolish in the front of my family and friends. But the people I love and who care about me stuck by me and helped me get through it all, and I'd like to take this opportunity to thank them again now for being tough and sticking by me. So now I'm rebuilding my life and for the want of better words 'I'm climbing back on the horse'. The stress of the situation I have found myself in has caused problems for me physically. I was putting on a brave act, but the tension came out in other ways, and that was to mess with my body. But it's not in my nature to give up, so I'm going to keep on fighting and not give up on what I want to do with my life.

Having a physical disability isn't easy to deal with. Some days it's damn hard and gets me down and I take it out on the people I'm closest to. It's true what people say that you strike about at the ones that you love the most. Every day is a battle, a challenge for me. But I face life head on and never give up on what I want to do. Some battles are worth fighting because it leads to better things and I wouldn't change anything with my life because the good things in my life far outweigh the bad.

If there were one bit of advice I could give anyone out there this would be it. 'Never give up on what you want to do in your life even when it seems impossible and out of reach. Nothing is impossible when you want it badly enough'.

Within 24 hours of the Bobsleigh disappointment Ruth is smiling again and ready to fight back

Chapter 11 – The Need for Speed

Steve

So it's settled. We're off to Silverstone race track. The first step is to take a look at the website and see if there are passenger high speed rides, which a quick look at their home page tells me that 'hot rides' looks promising. Another excellent sign is that there is a disabled access facility on the website – this is impressive as many sites haven't introduced this yet. They provide a special telephone number for disabled people that are having trouble navigating around the site. The 'hot ride' is in a Caterham 7 which is a great little traditional British two-seater open top sports car – tiny, but very fast. 0-60mph in 5.3 seconds and well over 120mph on the track should be plenty. Taking a look at the side of the Caterham in the pictures gives a moment of concern as to whether Ruth can lift herself in so I make sure that when I ring up I specifically ask.

"Disabled access is no problem" the chap on the other end of the booking line says.

"The main things are the height and weight restrictions, and the person needs enough upper body strength to lift themselves in and out of the seat". Ruth has plenty of strength in her arms and she'll have a couple of us there to help so I book up tickets for Ruth and myself. We have 11:20 and 11:30 slots. The car takes you around the South circuit at Silverstone which is part of the Formula 1 circuit itself. Three laps and about six miles. I bang off an email to Onno to see if he can join us that weekend – 26th January. We're trying to make a weekend of it for him as coming over form Amsterdam for 3 minutes in a car...

A week later Onno confirms and we're able to get him the 12:10 slot.

The Track
The first thing that hits you when you get to Silverstone is the size of the place. It's a while since the TV pictures of the muddy fields that passed as car parks in the old days with stranded cars – now the overall complex is pretty impressive. It's a bit weird coming here when there isn't a grand prix on – the place feels somewhat deserted even though there is a lot going on. We reach the gate and ask the guard where to go for the 'experiences' and he says "round to the left, two miles and over the bridge". That gives you an idea of the size. Onno comments that the place looks like an airport.

"They do have a runway for the drivers and others to fly in on in their private jets" Ruth adds.

The two miles turns out to be around the edge of the circuit and we keep looking out of for the bridge which eventually comes into view. The bridge takes us up over the track and down to the experience centre on the right hand side.

We park up (very good disabled parking) and as soon as we are inside and up to the counter we are greeted warmly by a charming lady called Beverley. "You're here for the hot ride" she smiles at Ruth and she already has our names ready. There is a form to sign in on and we have plenty of time to nose around. There is a shop with various merchandise from Silverstone which is quite cool and Ruth settles on a fleece, t-shirt and cap as mementos of the day. We get chatting with the guy in the shop and who it turns out has developed a new modified go-kart for disabled people which has a flappy paddle accelerator and brake similar to the gear change in an F1 car. Ruth talks animatedly about the times she had driven a similar, if more basic, go-kart and once we have deposited the goodies in the boot of the car I return to the shop by myself to talk about potential photos. It turns out they have a photographer that takes the F1 experience (you drive a baby F1 car on the track) photos and as a favour they will try and see if they can get a shot of Ruth in the car going round the track. Photography on the day is a paid extra, but not normally done for the hot rides. He'll see what he can do.

We head to the café which is quite neatly laid out for wheelchair access. We needn't have phoned ahead from the motorway services to check on the disabled loos in the experience centre itself as they are very well set up. As it gets closer to the time Beverley comes out to get us and Jof comes to organise the helmet for Ruth.

Ruth in the front seat of the Lotus

He explains that the Caterham is in for maintenance and they have switched to a brand new Lotus Elise S which is a supercharged car that is quite a bit faster than the Caterham. We tell Jof all about the reason behind the car ride and the failed Bobsleigh attempts and he assures us that the driver, Ben, will get Ruth's adrenalin pumping.

The staff here are so friendly and the fact that getting Ruth into the car takes longer, considering the slots are 10 minutes apart, is no issue. We aren't made to feel rushed at any point.

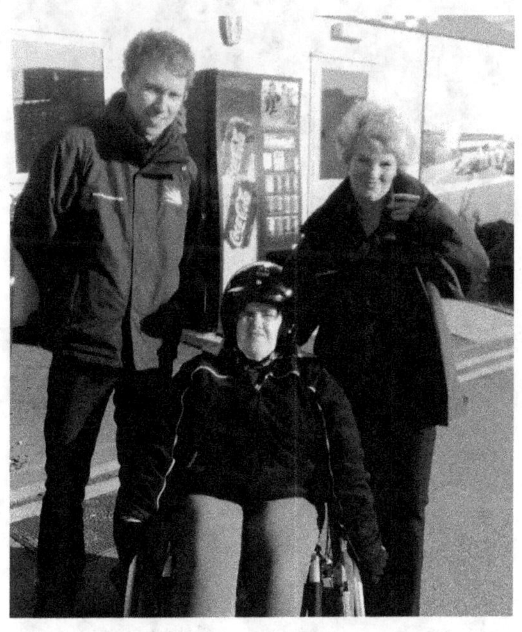

Jof Cox, Ruth, Beverley Harwood-Penn

The first challenge we find is that the Lotus' doors don't open as far out as a standard car so we can get Ruth's chair close but not right up next to the lip of the car. We manage to swing Ruth's legs over the edge and then slide slowly towards the seat.

We find we need to remove her helmet to get her into the seat but after a little juggling around she's in and Ben and Jof strap her in for the ride. The two lads are excellent and Ruth is very excited.

Doors on the Lotus not the easiest for disabled access –
but it certainly looks the part

Onno and I head for the hill by the bridge to takes photos and we can see the car fly past as Ruth goes round the track. I do hope the photographer can get a few good shots as from up here without a decent zoom we're not going to get any pictures that we can use.

Ruth
As soon as Ben has taken the car out of the car park and heads towards the track he floors it and we accelerate up to 100mph in a few hundred yards. I ask Ben if he can go any faster and immediately he puts his foot down. I'm loving this. The Lotus is low to the ground and it reminds me of how I used to feel in my sit-ski and my go kart. Like in my racing days by the second lap I am beginning to memorize the corners, the correct apexes and where the corner markers and poles are. Going as fast as we are I am getting great hip rotation, so much so that my shoes fall off in the middle of lap three – but I don't care! Here I am racing at Silverstone, shoes or no shoes. The third lap is over and Ben brings the car back towards the building. That was absolutely incredible and I just want Ben to turn the car around and go back out there.

Steve
Ruth is talking ten to a dozen as soon as the door opens. Getting her out of the car is not too bad as soon as we realise trying to get her straight into the chair is not going to happen. It's far simpler to let her slide out of the car onto the ground and then lift her up into the chair.

It's then straight into the car for me and we're off. I make the mistake of letting Ben know that Andy has a Tuscan (TVR) which is fast and he assures me that he won't disappoint in terms of speed. It takes two corners for my heart to start racing as although the straight line speed is familiar from the TVR, the cornering is something else. Onno commented afterwards that it was almost as if the car was an extension of Ben, that he knows every inch and I have to agree. He throws the car around the track drifting and sliding and I'm sure he deliberately takes the car onto the edges to give extra bumps and thrills. Every time he takes the car within inches of the pillars your brain says "he's going to hit it!" even though you know he won't.

Lap 1 is a rush and Lap 2, because you know what's coming in the corners you begin to relax a little. Then Ben steps it up for Lap 3 and you are literally bouncing off the chicane.

We have a chance for another coffee before Onno's turn and Ruth's on good form ribbing Onno that he shouldn't be too scared of the car. Ruth explains that while she was going around her shoes actually came off as the speed of the turns meant that her legs rotated quite a lot.

"I've found a cure for my legs not moving" she laughs. This draws a few worried looks from surrounding tables.

"The only challenge is that it does require going 125mph around corners in a racing car" I add.

"Oh yes." Ruth laughs. "Can't really do that in the office now can I?". Ruth explains that this is the first time in many years that she has had that much leg rotation. It was similar to when she used a sit-ski and the track felt quite a lot like when she did the slalom and giant slalom in skiing.

Onno heads out for his lap and we are joined by the manager of the experience centre who has popped out to have a chat with us to see that everything has gone well for our day. I leave Ruth chatting away and head into the shop where the team have sorted out the photos. The photographer is a genius as he has captured Ruth flying around a corner and the picture is stunning. They print it and mount it in a frame and give me the three certificates for the day.

Ruth, Onno and Lewis Hamilton

We say our goodbyes and head off back to Hemel Hempstead. The atmosphere in the car is fantastic and we are all raving about the day. We drop Ruth off and she gives Onno a tour of her flat.

"It's just not logic to have a disabled person's house half way up a very steep hill" he says. "and then there is the slope down to the front door as well".

"When you've waited twenty years for something to be allocated" Ruth replies "you take it".

Onno marvels at the kitchen with its lowered surfaces and Ruth's extensive movie collection (she has over 2,000) which lines her lounge walls. We say our goodbyes and leave Ruth to phone round all her friends and family to let them know about the day.

Ruth, a Lotus Elise S, 120mph

We head back home and we can't stop smiling.

"I think we've finally buried the ghost of the Bobsleigh" I say to Onno.

"I think we have" he smiles.

THE END

(With Ruth? Oh no it isn't, but for now that's your lot)

Chapter 12 – Lessons Learnt

As we spoke about the book we were asked by several people to compile all the hints and tips into a single chapter at the end so that it was easy to come back to the key lessons learnt.

We will be working with the charity on more projects in the future and would love to hear ideas from disabled people and carers that we can include. Send your ideas to mxpublishing@btinternet.com

- *When considering transport for a disabled person remember they will need to go into the front seat of the car – vital if you have a very tall lad like Andy 6'5" with you – and with taxis and hire cars specify an estate as its way faster than detaching the wheels every time.*

- *Hand luggage for the helper – you can't go wrong with a back-pack. You will, at many times need both hands to push the chair and within a few minutes any weight split across your arms will be uncomfortable. The back-pack is a lifesaver.*

- *Always have some backup food with you in the case of travelling with a vegetarian. A banana or a chocolate bar in the bag would have gone down a treat at that moment we found ourselves with no meal on the plane.*

- *Most disabled people in a chair develop strong upper body strength and are expert at how to move themselves in and out of their chair. 'Helping' them move can often actually be a hindrance so always ask first.*

- *Temperature regulation may be an issue for a disabled person. Especially important in extremely cold conditions make sure you have made provision to keep warm.*

- *When you are going shopping with a disabled person, first stop is to find a good, clean, working disabled toilet and use that place as a triangulation point. It saves a lot of time later.*

- *Choose a heavy set disabled person if you are planning on 'car park ticket discounting'.*

The final piece of advice we will remind you all of is to **'never assume'** when you're planning things with a disabled person. From getting on trains to online-check in there are so many everyday processes that we 'able-bodied' (a term Steve's not so keen on as many non-disabled people much less able than their disabled counterparts) take for granted and are either difficult or impossible for disabled people to follow.

Inspiring Stories

Ruth's story is wonderful and representative of the determination of many disabled people. Here is another inspirational story that we wanted to include in the book.

Amar Latif

Amar Latif (33) set out to be 'the blind guy who wanted to show people the world'. In 2005 he set up Traveleyes as the first commercial tour operator to specialise in holidays for visually impaired and sighted travelers. The sighted and visually impaired traveler journey together in the spirit of mutual independence with the latter acting as the 'eyes' for the former by providing visual descriptions.

Amar Latif – Entrepreneur

Amar lost his sight at the age of sixteen due to the genetic condition Retinitis Pigmentosa. He says the saddest thing about being blind is that he hasn't seen his mum's smile for more than sixteen years.

Amar is the winner of the inaugural Stelios Disabled Entrepreneur Award that's run by charity Leonard Cheshire Disability with Sir Stelios Haji-Ioannou, the founder of easyGroup. Stelios presented Amar with a cheque for £50,000 in November 2007 and Amar is using the money to grow Traveleyes internationally. He set up local phone numbers in Auckland , New York , Sydney and Toronto . As a result he has visually impaired and sighted travelers from America and Canada booked on to his holidays.

Amar and guide with lions in South Africa

Rather like the adventurer, author and social observer James Holman (15.10.1786 - 29.07.1857) who was known as 'The Blind Traveler' Amar, from proudly held Glaswegian roots, has always enjoyed adventure, along with independent world travel and has put on his kilt and walked across continents.

Amar has a degree in Maths, Statistics and Finance, BSc, (Strathclyde University 1997) and is a qualified Management Accountant CMA 2001. He studied maths in Canada for one undergraduate year.

Amar adapted the Lonely Planet guides to audio format - he has now joined with the Lonely Planet and has exclusive use of the travel guides for Traveleyes visually impaired traveler.

Cuba 2007 Group Photo

Amar plans his trips using a tactile map. He pushes a button for the country he wants to research and the National Geographic map tells him the country details.

He directed Sightseeing Blind a documentary set in Florence for Channel 4 and featured in the BBCs first series of Beyond Boundaries when he trekked 200 miles across Nicaragua. He was armed with a Braille compass, water and food rations and a tent. Added to this he had to push a wheelchair user.

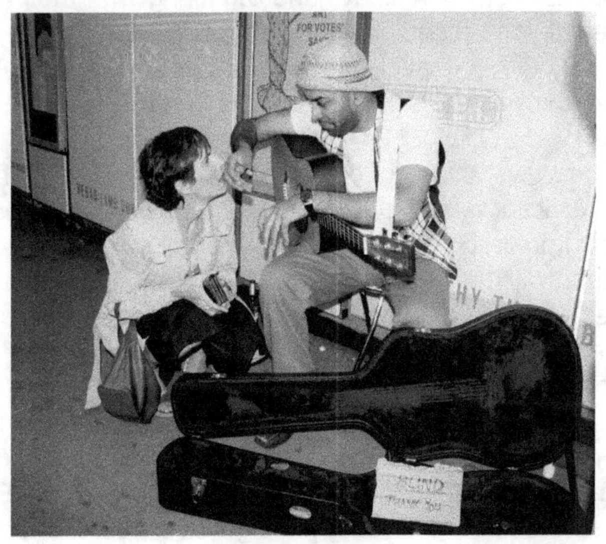

Amar with Tasmin Greig in Love Soup

What Amar says

"Amar, a Scotsman from proudly-held Glaswegian roots, now based in Leeds , said: "I set up Traveleyes as from an early age I always suspected there was a stunningly beautiful, diverse, fragrant and musical world waiting out there that's just aching to be touched, tasted, tried, tested, plunged into and explored. Traveleyes was the medium I created in order to render this dream a reality, not only for blind traveler , but for sighted traveler too – especially those who may have long searched for holiday experiences offering greater social, sensory and cultural variety and enhanced personal fulfillment.

"Visually impaired people are often expected to accept limitations on their holidays and tag along with their family or friends, or accept other limitations on where they can travel to. On a Traveleyes holidays they are completely independent as the sighted buddy is in no way a carer.

'We're always thinking of new holidays and will offer a South African safari in November 2008. On the safari the visually impaired person will hold the tail of a one year old lion that will guide them through the safari area as the sighted traveler describes the sights. I did it earlier this year and it was the first time I'd seen a lion and a great experience.

"There are some great facilities for blind people in South Africa . The botanical gardens in Cape Town have a Braille trail, so there is no need for a sighted guide. Visitors can spend hours along following a rope path through the gardens, stopping every now and again to read the Braille boxes for information about the surrounding flowers and plants. Blind people don't often get the chance to spend so much time alone.

"Before setting up Traveleyes I worked as an accountant, culminating in my being in charge of teams of accountants in large corporations. Initially, whenever I went to graduate interviews, I began to see a pattern. Often, a general lack of knowledge about disability on the part of employers led many to think that the whole business of employing disabled people was somehow just too risky.

"This explained the shockingly high unemployment rates among disabled people of working age in the UK . After a number of initial failures at graduate interviews, I developed my own approach, which entailed my taking an active role from the outset. I would start by giving a short presentation about my blindness and explain why it does not hamper my performance in the workplace. The effect was remarkable. Job offers quickly followed my adoption of this tactic.

"I really believe that the positive approach is the way to overcome the fear, prejudice and misconception that often stand in the way of disabled people. Many disabled people may, like me, wish to become entrepreneurs, but no one should be forced into self-employment by a lack of employment opportunity in the job market."

Channel 4 Director

The Sighted and Blind Traveler packs

Amar has prepared packs for sighted travelers as most of them have never met a blind person before. It includes such information as how best to give visual descriptions i.e. the view at Niagara Falls . There is also one for the blind traveler so they understand the needs of the sighted traveler.

How to book - and website address

Travelers book online at www.traveleyes.co.uk - or phone Amar and the team in their Leeds office to book.

Activities

Travelers can choose to simply relax, or they could do cookery courses in Italy. Dance salsa and sky-dive in Cuba. Paraglide and do water sports in Fuerteventura.

Some revealing quotes about Amar and his public speaking:

"I was delighted to learn that you recently won the Business and Entrepreneurial category of the 'Outstanding Young Person of the World' Award at the Junior Chamber International World Congress in Vienna. As Scotland's First Minister, I was particularly pleased to see that someone who was brought up and educated in Scotland has been the recipient of such a prestigious award.."
(Jack McConnell, former First Minister of Scotland).

"Without question we have received some excellent feedback from the guests who attended the dinner. It is clear that they were enthralled, captivated and inspired. You could have heard a pin drop as the audience clung on to every word Amar uttered."
(Project Manager, Venturefest 2007)

"I just wanted to thank you for speaking to us at Barclays capital. It was great to meet you and we have had some really positive feedback from the attendees, all of whom found your talk incredibly motivating. As a result we have boosted or Disability Awareness Forum membership significantly and we will be able to build on this for future events."
(Equality & Diversity Director, Barclays Capital)

"This has been the most inspiring and touching presentation I have ever experienced in my twenty five years of working in this company."
(Director of BT)

"I've been totally inspired by everything Amar said tonight. Now I know it's not impossible for me to become a pilot".
(16-year old boy from inner-city school).

Amar speaks on a range of themes: entrepreneurial, inspirational, his own life, world travel, equality and diversity. His affiliations span widely across every ethnicity and   creed. Here is a true 'free spirit', celebrating a positive, vibrant, forward-looking, multi-cultural world. For Amar, blindness is a challenge to which he responds on a daily basis:

A final word from Amar:

> "Whilst every year my eyesight becomes more restricted……every year, the sky becomes higher and the horizon becomes wider, and more tantalizing and more magnificent in the hidden mysteries…..all waiting to be revealed. I'm the blind guy….who wants to show you the world!"

Appendix 1 - Email from the Tracks

"Hello Steve,

I don't think you could do that. At least not
with no experienced driver and brakeman. The
so-called taxi bobs have a driver and a
brakeman and take two passengers in the middle.
That's something you can do on almost any
bobsleigh and luge track.

Winterberg would be the nearest track to Great
Britain, in America there are the tracks at
Lake Placid, Park City and Calgary.

Contact the tracks and try to explain to them
what you would like to do.

All the best
regards
Ingeborg"

Appendix 2 – Hot Rides

Location: Silverstone Race Track, near Northampton (around 1.5 hours from London, 1 hour Birmingham)

Website: www.silverstone.co.uk

Cost: £39 (allow £75-£100 to include a decent memento of the day like a cap or a t-shirt, breakfast, lunch and dinner)

Car: Caterham 7 or Lotus Elise S

Speeds: 120-140mph

Laps: 3

Length of time: Around 6-10 minutes but the build up is all part of the day out.

**You Too Can Do Health
Olive Hickmott, Sarah Knighton**

Stunning book from two leading NLP master practitioners on addressing health issues. Both authors battled serious illness and in Sarah's case her cancer finally took her just after the book was completed in November. Originally given just months to live, Sarah battled on for twelve years helping and inspiring other sufferers to take their illnesses head on. A truly inspirational book and a must read for anyone involved with health and wellness. A fitting legacy for an incredible woman.

Seeing Spells Achieving
Andrew Bendefy, Olive Hickmott

"For anyone with dyslexia, and any parent or someone involved in learning, education and health, these processes of visualisation integrate so well with existing teaching methods and they do give us all another tool, a new choice for growth and development to achieve new goals"
National Family Learning Network

**The Gift – Real Life NLP
Kirsty McKinnon**

"It can be used in so many different ways from helping businesses to giving people the skills they need do better at school, while also being useful for treating phobias and helping people lose weight or stop smoking".
Daily Record

Succeed In Sport
Jackie Wilkinson

Five times British Archery champion Jackie Wilkinson brings us the secrets to enhanced performance across all sports. Contributions from leading Olympians and leading athletes from Athletics, Running, Golf, Karate, Archery, Show Jumping, Cricket and more.

Process and Prosper
Wendy Harrington

Amazing motivational book from Necrotizing Faciitis survivor
Wendy.

www.ingramcontent.com/pod-product-compliance
Lightning Source LLC
Chambersburg PA
CBHW070817240726
48654CB00007B/390